The Guide to Durban, South Africa (the Sharks, the Most Beautiful Pier in the World, the White Rhino, the African Safari, the Hippos and the Zulu Dancers) from Pearl Escapes 2017

By Pearl Howie

Copyright © Pearl Howie 2019

First Edition

The moral right of the author has been asserted

The right of Pearl Howie to be identified as the author of this book has been asserted by her in accordance with the Copyright, Design & Patents Act, 1988.

ISBN: 978-0-244-48623-5

All rights reserved. Apart from any use permitted under UK copyright law, no part of this publication may be reproduced, stored or transmitted in any form or by any means without the prior permission in writing of the publisher or in the case of reprographic production in accordance with the terms of licences issued by the Copyright Licensing Agency.

Published by Pearl Escapes
www.pearlescapes.co.uk
pearl@pearlescapes.co.uk

Also by the Author

Camino de la Luna Series (self-help/travel)

(Available as full colour paperbacks and colour pdf eBooks with photos. The first few audiobooks are out now.)

Japan Is Very Wonderful
free Feeling Real Emotions Everyday
Camino de la Luna – Take What You Need
Camino de la Luna – Unconditional Love
Camino de la Luna – Forgiveness
Camino de la Luna – Compassion and Self Compassion
Camino de la Luna – Courage
Camino de la Luna – Truth
Camino de la Luna – Reconciliation

Other Titles

Pearl Escapes Guide to Healing 2019 - Massage, Meditation, Spa Treatments, Teachers, Practices and Places (Seventh Edition)

The Guide to Spa Breaks and Escapes from Pearl Escapes (various editions)

Meditation for Angry People

The Wee, The Wound And The Worries: My Experience Of Being A Kidney Donor

Love And The Perfect Wave (romantic novel)

Pearl Escapes Mini-Guides

My mini-guides attempt to give you the hotel, spa, restaurant and the rest, just the bullet, the escape in a box I dreamt of when I first began Pearl Escapes:-

Venice
Johannesburg, South Africa
Sacromonte, Granada, Spain   La Paz, Baja, Mexico
Ignacio Springs and Guerrero Negro, Baja, Mexico
Barcelona   Zadar, Croatia
Marrakech, Morocco   Paris
Little Italy In New York   London Spas and Massage
Bath Spa   Hong Kong
Yangshuo, China   Shanghai, China
Huangshan/Yellow Mountain   Beijing, China
Iceland   Brockenhurst, the New Forest
Florida   Key Largo
Clearwater   Orlando Convention Center
Naples, Florida, Big Cypress and the Everglades
Swimming With Wild Manatees In Crystal River, Florida
Chianciano Terme, Tuscany   Livorno, Florence, Viareggio
Spas, Escapes and Breaks in England (and in Wales)
The Lake District (Ullswater)   Las Vegas
Cozumel, Cancun, Mexico   Vero Beach, Florida

For
Mo Diakite,
Ricardo Marmitte
and his brothers,
and especially
Lucas Mthenjane
and dance partner,
for bringing Africa to me, so that I could go to Africa.

Contents

Also by the Author 2
Introduction 8
Flight - Johannesburg to King Shaka International Airport 10
The Shark Tour - KwaZulu-Natal Sharks Board
Maritime Centre of Excellence (KZNSB), Durban 12
Coastlands Musgrave Hotel, Durban, South Africa 13
The Most Beautiful Pier in the World - Umhlanga Rocks 16
Protea Hotel by Marriott Durban Umhlanga 18
The Place Where They "Saved"
The White Rhino - Hluhluwe–Imfolozi 19
The African Safari - Leopard Mountain Safari Lodge 21
The Hippo House - Sandpiper Guesthouse 30
St Lucia 33
The Zulu Dancers - PheZulu 39
The Gandhi Moment – Near Pietermaritzburg 39
Protea Hotel by Marriott Hilton 40
How I Got There and Getting Around 41
The Details and the Rest 43
About the Author 48
Thank You 49

Introduction

When I first started travelling, and visiting spas and having massages, I justified the expense by writing my guides. Then I set off on my wilder adventures and, although I kept track, made notes and kept journals, I was in no doubt that the whole thing was for me – I had no illusions that I was helping others or that I was doing it for the guidebooks. In seeking to follow my heart, live my dreams and heal myself, I went to many wonderful places.

What I learned is that my heart will always lead me to rediscover myself, to heal and see everything in a new light, especially the stories I've told myself about my life and the people in it. And this magical, selfish pilgrimage brought me to moments when I knew I had to come back and be with the people I loved, and ultimately share these incredible adventures with the world – with anyone who needs a little help to escape.

I've learned that if it is in our nature to help others, to be kind, generous, to write, sing or dance, then by setting ourselves free of any notion of serving others we come back to the truth, and to our most natural way of being, and serving.

\|/

When I first started dreaming of this wild adventure,

(what would become my "Camino de la Luna,") I would have said "There's only place left on my bucket list... Africa." But which Africa? Namibia kept calling, the safest of destinations (as soon as you get away from the South African border,) and Botswana, famous for hippos (a must see on my African safari wish list,) another safe option. Then one day walking in the woods I hugged a tree (as you do) and it said "Go to South Africa." Over a year later I had travelled so much, waiting for the temperature in Southern Africa to cool so I could venture there, that I said, "I don't really need to go anymore, I've done so many of the things I wanted to do in Africa." And yet, it hung in there, this lifetime dream and this whisper from the forest... and then I saw an article about Durban in South Africa and I knew where I was meant to go. (But to get there I had to go through Johannesburg – which is in my sister Pearl Escapes guide.)

This guide is a little different to my previous "escapes in a box," as I've put the details at the end. If you want to read the full story, it's in my book "Camino de la Luna – Reconciliation," available with and without pictures, in eBook and paperback and someday, in audio book form. If you just want the quick guide, the rest of the story is in my mini-guide to Johannesburg, South Africa.

Flight - Johannesburg to King Shaka International Airport

I don't know what I'm going to do in Durban or why I'm going, I've tried to book onto a shark tour tomorrow but they need a minimum of four people and the people they had for tomorrow just cancelled – oh well, the right thing will come along.

I'm glad I didn't book my flight, glad I can say "Shaab Shaab," (Okay – which also means "Thank You," "Please," "Hello," "Goodbye," "Yes," and "No,") to my driver and glad I am travelling light enough to not have to check my bag in. I bounce around between the boards announcing flights and kiosks selling tickets. I'm also trying to work in my BA air miles, either to spend them or get them. It's a bit of a mess – a lot of the flights are code shares, but some that go at exactly the same time aren't – some of them, especially the cheaper ones are already sold out. There are a few first class tickets left, nope, they're sold out too. In the end I wind up on a flight in an hour or so with a not too expensive ticket and, although I can't use my BA airmails, I end up getting a few more.

South Africa's kind of funny when it comes to queuing. English people could usually win an Olympic gold medal (if there was one) for queuing, we do not break and if someone tries to cut in line they may not be confronted but will be given a death stare. In France, good luck. In Japan they can queue in five or six parallel lanes and all will be in order. But in most airports around the world I find people are pretty "English" in their queuing, maybe it's all the security and rules? But here in South Africa, well in Jo'burg, loads of people are running into the airport transparently late for their flights, and they just cut in, and everyone lets them, and no one cares because, you know, obviously if they're running they need to get through security to their gate. It reminds me of that time I was running in a Mexican airport and I flew past an American guy walking – the security guy held his hand out for a passport and boarding pass and I flashed him mine as I flew past and the American drawled (because he's American and I love that word) "I thought I was first."

Here I walk into the women's toilets and there's a woman standing with a mop, smiling so hard, "Welcome to my office" she says. (There's no tipping, she's just supremely happy.) And in that moment I am so jealous of her, of her joy. I wish I could be as happy as this lady working in Jo'burg cleaning toilets.

It's so easy to look at someone's outside - I have money, enough for now, enough to go to any country pretty much in the world, I have time, enough to go to any country pretty much in the world, I have all the freedom that I wanted, and yet, my heart is broken and money can't buy true happiness. Money helps, because I can go where I want and maybe find somewhere that helps me heal, but I have learned that in order to be me, to practise what I believe, to live how I want, I may have to give up the people who mean most to me in the world. But deeper than that, what cuts right through, is knowing that if the people who mean the most to me don't accept me the way I am, then pretending to be what they want me to be won't work either. It will destroy me just so that they can love a mask, an effigy that isn't real.

The Shark Tour - KwaZulu-Natal Sharks Board Maritime Centre of Excellence (KZNSB), Durban

Hey, I got an email from the Sharks Board about the tour:

Dear Pearl,

I have tried to call but your cell phone goes unanswered. Please note tomorrow's boat tour (08/09/2017) is going ahead as planned. You are required to be at Wilson's Wharf at 06:00am for 06:30am. Payment of R350,00 per person will be required on board the boat. Your skipper will be Frank Mtolo. Please use Entrance 1 when accessing Wilson's Wharf.

Regards,
Sithembele
www.shark.co.za

Great, some more people must have booked on! I book a plush looking hotel near Wilson's Wharf, looks like I could even walk from there. There are lots of nice guesthouses but I'm getting in late and leaving early, so a hotel's probably best.

Coastlands Musgrave Hotel, Durban, South Africa

The front's nice but it's a bit more basic when you get to the rooms (okay, I've been spoilt in the last two places). My driver is really cool, gives me lots of local info, but tells me to take cabs to the wharf, especially at that time in the morning.

I'm twitchy again and ask to move rooms, but the next one isn't that great either – so I end up moving back.

I hate getting in late, but it's not the kind of place where there's a lot to do if I'd arrived earlier. I just need to get my head down and get some sleep before the tour in the morning.

I get that look from my cab driver when I tell him I was thinking of walking here before sunrise. Once we reach the wharf it's pretty safe, there's a little security office and, although they can't direct me to where exactly I get the boat, it's a nice enough spot to hang out and watch the sun rise. I meet the other people for the tour before we find our guy, and then we're onto a luxury boat and our captain is explaining the ropes to us.

The other tourists on the boat are from Jo'burg. When

they ask where I've been, I tell them I loved Maropeng.

They're shocked. "We don't go there. No, that's not safe."

Seemed pretty perfect to me.

On the upside it's a gorgeous morning and one of the nicest boats I've ever been on.

On the downside it seems I was mislead by the magazine article about Durban and this tour; it's not that it's that unusual for them to get sharks out of the nets, it's that when they do the shark is dead. It's around 300 sharks a year, but unless they get to it within a few minutes it'll die. This is why they normally have several shark dissections at their centre each week. It makes sense, they use the dead animal for scientific research and to educate people about sharks. But no, I don't personally want to go see a shark dissection.

We learn all about the history of the nets and Durban, and surfing in Durban, but I don't get the vibe of this city yet.

We are blessed with dolphins, bursting out from each side of the boat (too fast for me to catch on my camera – although I try) even the skipper is blown away by how many, and no dead sharks today.

And then it's back in to Durban.

It was lovely but I feel, once again, what am I doing here? Where am I going? I'm back so early I have time to chill out in my hotel room, which is actually rather lovely, shower, even call a good friend in Paris who's been helping me set up my book tour (in fairness she's doing everything) and chat. I often say that, even if I just help one person, anything I do is worth it, and it's what I say to her when she worries that not a lot of a people have said they'll come. "Maybe I'm just coming for you." I say. When my Zumba classes were really quiet in London, I'd always try to think, 'This is someone's mother, sister, daughter, brother... so try to give them everything I would wish someone would give my mother, sister, daughter, brother.'

And then I enjoy tea and cake by the sort of pool hot tub thing (I don't go in) and appreciate it because the cake is really out of this world and the staff at the café are just heart-warmingly kind. How can I make this trip work? What can I give myself, me, the love of my own life to make me happy?

The beach?

Well, I also book a car from Umhlanga Rocks (pronounced Umshlanga) at the other end of Durban, (and am glad I have a cab to drive me across town until I get used to my new car), and then head to the famous Oyster Box Hotel to see if I can get a massage too.

The Most Beautiful Pier in the World - Umhlanga Rocks

Yeah it does.

It has what some have called the most beautiful pier in the world, and of course that lighthouse, stacks of world class hotels, spas, bars and restaurants. It's a cool spot. Sadly The Oyster Box doesn't have time for a massage, but they kindly take my bags so I'm free to roam the hotel (which has no vegan food), they apologise. And give me ice water by the pool while I try to decide where to eat lunch and where to stay, using their WiFi.

In the end food is easy, I stroll up the road, past someone who reminds me "The best revenge is to live well", (well, I don't believe in revenge but I like the sentiment). Durban is sometimes referred to as the largest Indian city outside India and they have a special dish called a bunny – curry served up in a loaf of bread. So I hit a bunny shop for a vegan bunny, which absolutely hits the spot.

Durban was also where Gandhi arrived and lived in South Africa when he started his career – apparently he couldn't get a job in India or England.

I'm not entirely sure I'd call it the most beautiful pier in the world, but beauty, like most things, is in the eye of the beholder.

I've found a resort up the road that specialises in

traditional massage – they even have rituals and things, so I'm going to take my new car up there and check it out. In the meantime I wander around and check out the hotels here, I'm becoming fond of the feel of the Protea chain, it's a Marriott but still, they've made them South African. When I wander around the one right on the street with cafes and bars I'm in love. It doesn't feel like a chain hotel, more like a boutique.

And I catch a little sun on the beach, where the whole world comes to relax and chill out.

I'm glad I relaxed on the beach because I'm nervous again picking up my hire car. (Is it because it's South Africa, or because it's a hire car company, or because of all those times I got hit from behind by a fee I didn't expect, or because it's already got scratches on it?) I'm nervous pulling out of the parking lot, I almost want to turn round, give it back and just stay here (come on, I never would have booked the car if I'd known how nice Umhlanga is) and nervous as I pull out and get beeped because it's a busy junction.

The hotel and spa has really different ratings on Tripadvisor, I'm nervous leaving my bags in the car, walking through the massive hotel (it's like all the enormous native American casinos in the US) and, while they do have time for a massage, it's not a relaxing experience. I put my valuables in their weak ass lockers and my heart starts beating double time immediately. I wish I could relax, wish I could enjoy, but no, it's crazy, oceans of people coming for some traditional African healing, and the massage is pretty average as far as I can tell between freaking out about my STUFF, and the noises of OTHER people through the traditional African walls. I want to tell her to just STOP, I want to leave, to get out of there. Finally it's over and I'm heading back, standing in the car park just long enough to watch the sun set over the African hills (this hotel does have a nice view) and going as fast as I can to try and get back to my spot, my Protea hotel before dark. And then I can't figure out parking, the street is packed, I can't find the hotel parking lot, so I put it behind the hotel where the ticket machine is broken, but as me and the guy on the gate figure, a lost ticket is the same price as an overnight stay, so I'll just pay for a lost ticket in the morning.

Protea Hotel by Marriott Durban Umhlanga

I don't go down to the beach in the dark, I'm not that brave, or stupid, I still don't know which.

I roam the cafes and bars, soaking up the atmosphere, the music, the food, before collapsing in my lovely Protea hotel room, where only the little window opens, because apparently you can't be trusted to go out on the balcony (unless you book one of the bigger rooms at the end of the corridor where they do trust you to use your balcony and not fall off).

As I said it's a lovely room, but the view is of the

building site next door, so I head down to the beach with my breakfast. I dip, but don't swim, there are strong currents, but we are protected from the sharks.

Where next?

Wherever I'm going I need essentials, I need toothpaste. Luckily there are all kinds of shops and even guys selling fruit in the park – a bit of everything. But when I pop into the pharmacy I can't choose toothpaste – because none of the ten or twenty brands has a price on it. I ask an assistant. She asks me which toothpaste I'm interested in out loud, then in hushed tones tells me it'll all be cheaper in the supermarket down the street.

The Place Where They "Saved" The White Rhino - Hluhluwe–Imfolozi

I'm not that far from the Hluhluwe–Imfolozi (pronounced Shuh...wey...wey-Imfolozi) Park (or rather parks) often credited as the oldest game reserve in Africa, and the place where they "saved" the white rhino. It's now got the biggest population of white rhino anyway – sounds like it's worth a look.

I must admit, I'm nervous to go into the reserves here. In Sri Lanka in Yala just one half day safari drive was enough to wreck my body for two days, and the other tourists who I met there told me Africa was much tougher. Mind you, staying in Yala was incredible – maybe I can find a nice place to stay in or near the reserve?

I find Leopard Mountain Safari Lodge. There's another place, much, much cheaper, where they have rescued animals, but the bathroom is shared and outside (I can do that in Spain I've discovered, but there are snakes here). Follow your heart, do the right thing, forget about the money, I tell myself and so I'm booking one night at Leopard Mountain because it's all they have available and that's the plan, that's where next.

All I have to do is get the car out of the car park and drive a few hours north east in daylight.

I struggle to get the car out of the car park. They don't understand why I'd leave the car without a ticket and it's gonna cost more than I thought. 'Here it comes,' I think, 'this is where you get ripped off.'

The guy goes off for ages, so long that I'm sitting in a hot car with the day ticking away and I'm thinking, just pay the guy... then he comes back and waves me through the barriers. "I can't find the boss," he says, "don't worry about it."

Where's that humility, trust and compassion I discovered in Sri Lanka?

As I fight my way out of town and onto a lonely road, there is but one car in front of me, maybe a taxi, maybe a driving school – the huge sign on it reads "Eagle", I am in the right place at the right time.

It's a long drive, and I soon discover that my food choice on South Africa's highways is a vegetarian WIMPY burger, pretty much obsolete in the UK these days.

It's food.

The African Safari - Leopard Mountain Safari Lodge

It's actually not in Hluhluwe–Imfolozi Park but in a separate private reserve "next door" called Manyoni. I'm not sure what I think yet about private reserves.

I love them.

I am the only car on the road (which will probably get scary in a minute) but wow, I am the only car on the road and the scenery is everything I ever dreamed Africa would be.

And I turn the corner and am in front of a giraffe.

I'm in wonder and a little bit of confusion. The signs to the different lodges are pretty good, except that at one point I'm not quite sure if I am on the road or have turned off accidentally. I am staring at another animal when I turn my head and a Leopard Mountain jeep is sitting behind me, the guide grinning at my reaction. I'm on the right track.

I'm still in awe of the Lodge, or rather lodges.

It's traditional style. With air con and floor to ceiling glass windows for the view, even in the bathroom where I have two sinks, a shower in front of the glass windows and, on the other side of the glass is a small dipping pool on my "hut" long verandah. (The loo is small and separate, thank goodness). I have a four poster bed which would make anyone narcoleptic, chairs, a hammock, all kinds of goodies... the only thing, they warn me, is that I shouldn't leave any food in the room as they're having a big problem with mice through the whole reserve. I hand over my stash of veganish grub I've picked up along the way. They don't blink or look down at it.

Would I like afternoon tea? It's all included. So I sit in the lounge and sigh at the view, racking my brain for what I have to do or remember for my game drive. I've brought a separate camera on this trip, just in case my phone craps out again. I have bug lotion, sun tan lotion... and then I just stop and eat cookies and drink tea and sigh at the view.

Our guide, Alex, is brilliant, and lets me sit in the front passenger seat (I'm anticipating a rough ride), but even he doesn't seem to be finding many animals. The high point (apart from some far off rhino spotted by the lady behind us who has incredibly sharp eyes) is a dung beetle casing.

Wow. (Okay, it doesn't really do it for me.) But the ride is smooth and eventually we spot some white rhino close up. I learn that there is no white rhino or black rhino, white is just a mistranslation or mispronunciation of wide. Basically it's wide rhino and less wide rhino we're looking for – they also happen to be peaceable (wide) and aggressive (less wide) -

you recognise a black rhino because it's running AT you.

On this reserve they've taken the action of cutting off the rhinos' horns, to prevent poaching. It's working. Alex tells us they've lost no rhino here since they started. It's expensive, and they grow back, but they don't lose rhino.

I ask him about a walking tour, which I saw on the hotel's website. He shakes his head, not worth it at the moment, better to stay in the jeep. There are no windows and we're basically sitting outside anyway (which is why they also pack blankets for us on the jeep).

I'm aching to see a big cat in the wild (although I don't even dream of seeing a leopard after Sri Lanka) and Alex sets his sights on finding us cheetah when it gets dark. They're easier to spot in the dark because their eyes glint in the headlights. (It goes like this, look for elephants in the day, never at night because they can be very dangerous, at night you look for cheetah and other animals with reflective eyes.) We see a family of cheetah and my life is complete.

It was a slow start, but now we celebrate. With proper gin and tonics and vegan snacks. My cup runneth over. If this is safari African style I'm sold. My body doesn't hurt, the drive is smooth and the chef is cooking me a special vegan dinner back at the lodge. And I have a blanket.

We take our time coming back. We haven't seen lions or elephants, (but hey, I came for the rhino and got cheetahs too – I'm happy). The lady with the sharp eyes and her husband were going to take a night tour but they're not sure it's worth it, it's slow tonight.

Then we turn a corner and run into a herd of elephants.

We proceed with great caution.

Mice are running everywhere, and then all of a sudden Alex stops, there's a baby hare in our path that doesn't want to move. While the mice flee, this baby hare does not know what to do with the headlights and just keeps hopping along directly in front of us. We're going to be very late back. But because we're going slow we also see other night treats; a bush baby in the trees and a nightjar comfy up there too.

"I'm going to be in so much trouble with the chef," Alex says. "We'd better get back."

And then we run into a kill.

We're at the bottom of a riverbed, the jeep bouncing, when the headlights catch the carcass. We stop. The light has scared the animals that killed it and are stripping it down (it's a kudu Alex thinks), but when we stop and wait we hear them in the trees and on the bank around us. Hyenas. Their calls are night calls, ghostly and eerie in the dark. We listen for a moment, Alex reckons there are about seven of them, two packs, maybe fighting with each other over the kill. But what took it down in the first place? It would be unusual for hyenas to take down a kudu. A leopard? We hear a leopard up in the tree. Perhaps it took down the kudu and then the hyenas have challenged it?

My phone dies. I pull out my second camera, it dies too. Clearly I am meant to just be here, just feel this moment.

Alex radios in. The woman back in the office is frustrated he's so late. He says we're going to be at least another half an hour. "I can give you twenty minutes," she says.

He fills her in on the situation. There's a pause. "Enjoy." she says.

The night noises are getting louder, one or two hyena return to the carcass and start stripping off the meat.

"Let's turn out all the lights and see how close they get," he says.

We're sitting in pitch black with the sounds of hyenas and a leopard growling up in the tree above us. Sometimes the hyenas fight, or threaten the leopard and each other. I am in an open topped jeep. My blood is bubbling with adrenaline.

"I will trust and not be afraid."

"I will trust and not be afraid."

I have to remind myself to breathe.

Alex flashes on the light to see just how close the hyenas have come. There is one beside me, four or five feet away, looking at me. I am a piece of flesh. I can sense this animal thinking, could he get away with it? I am a soft, easy piece of flesh, but there's a lot of metal here too.

I am meat.

He tracks back (I think it's a he), there's a definite she here too, pregnant and possibly hurt. She's eating when the others are hiding, maybe she didn't get there before or they're letting her eat more, perhaps the danger we represent is nothing compared to her need for food.

The leopard is high up, still making noises, but the fight we came in on has quieted down.

Alex turns out the lights again and we sit, as they keep calling. How could I ever have thought of the hyena as a bottom feeder, it's clearly a powerful predator, how could I ever have thought it wasn't a worthy animal to be reckoned with? This is a fierce fighter, a king of the jungle in its own right. A pack animal, sure, but even on its own a dangerous creature to cross paths with.

When we finally get back Alex disappears to be debriefed, this is something that just doesn't happen, they're usually lucky to even see a hyena, so they need as much detail as possible for scientific study, they even ask us for all of our photos and recordings. They're shocked when I tell them my cameras died. I shrug. Everything happens perfectly and the moments in the jeep are seared in my brain.

Because I'm alone Alex joins me for dinner – we eat fast, it's late and we're going to go out early in the morning again to see if there's any more activity around the kill. Eventually he walks me back to my lodge (no one walks around alone here at night). "I'm so tired," I say, "I might just lay out and sleep in my hammock on the verandah."

He shakes his head. "Don't do that. A woman was killed by a leopard in a hammock in Kruger." Apparently she was working there.

I have a few hours in my room before a 5am wake up call. I also have to pack up my bag, because check out is whilst we're on our morning game drive (or could be if we come across some more good stuff). It will still be dark so he'll come get me. My room is amazing and I curl up in the bed and pass out.

Then I am 100% awake. There's a noise. An animal noise. "Please God," I say, "let it be a mouse."

My body is rigid. All the adrenaline from the hyenas is back. "Don't move." I tell myself, "Don't make a sound". The nets around the four poster bed are no protection, no comfort. Would a snake make a sound? Slowly I make sense of my surroundings, here's the bed, here's the bathroom, where is the noise?

It's coming from the verandah. Outside, thank God. From the dipping pool. I am terrified, but what if it IS a leopard, on the other side of the glass...? I edge off the bed, reaching for my glasses. I creep towards the bathroom, until I can make out the dipping pool in the moonlight.

Nyala, a female antelope, drinking. Relief and joy. It looks up and flees. I head back to bed, and when it wakes me again I creep and watch once more.

The early morning call is early (it does take some time to get back to sleep each time with the adrenaline from the night!) and a little unnecessary, because they decide to give the other guests a chance to get out and see the kill first.

In the daylight the hyena is still daunting and it's a thrill, especially for the other guests, because they're a rare animal to see, especially this close, but none of it is as visceral as it was last night.

…apart from looking again at the riverbeds where we were driving and feeling the shock and the thrill of 'What if we'd hit those rocks and turned over?', a human in a car with metal around it is one thing, but a bleeding human on the floor… I don't think those hyena or that leopard would have been able to resist.

Our beautiful morning is broken with a break for hot chocolate and also for "bush toilet", peeing behind a rock and hoping there's no snakes there.

A mother and baby elephant are a real treat, and we see an awful lot of warthogs – the only animal able to defecate and run at the same time (if you'll ignore my really bad joke about Paula Radcliffe in Athens).

Alex also teaches us about an oversized thorn – an insect makes its home inside and somehow forces the tree to keep growing the thorn larger and larger.

I lose concentration. I want breakfast.

I'm not sure I have it in me to make it out for the other morning excursion - a trip to the hide, but the sharp eyed couple from last night gee me along, so I am back on the jeep, where we get quite the show of zebra on the way. They don't just rest their heads on each others backs, they're watching them.

The hide even has its own toilet although, despite the mod cons, given the choice I would have curled up back in my own bed, but I'm already checked out of my room.

There isn't much to see, but we're not particularly quiet. They even play back the recording of last night's animal noises. Even in the light and heat of day (and in the hide,) it makes my heart race.

Across the water a heron sits, taking me back to Wimbledon, to the moment where I understood the difference between the desire of my ego; to survive, and the desire of my soul; to explore, to soar, and to a moment when I could feel the heron take flight on the other side of the water. Now I am in South Africa, on safari and warthog are playing on the other side of the water. I am so grateful for my life, for this journey, for everything that has brought me here, even the worst moments.

"Do you mind if we go back," they ask. It's so hot out here. It's wonderful to go back and be escorted to the spa lodge where I finally have my traditional African healing massage in peace and quiet, the only sounds and the only sights (when I do open my eyes) the valley below the Leopard Mountain Lodge.

"Where are you going next?" they asked me at reception.

I'm thinking maybe St Lucia where they have a lot of hippo, and there's another town close by.

"No," they say, "you want to stay in St Lucia, but it's busy, let us..." and so, by the time I get back from my massage they've already booked me a room in a guesthouse in St Lucia.

I could get used to living like this, if it weren't for the early starts.

The Hippo House - Sandpiper Guesthouse

I take a wrong turn, but I don't just keep going. Maybe it's the satnav, maybe it's me misreading it, but I am on a lonely, rocky road and decide this can't be the way to St Lucia.

I'm glad I followed the lodge's advice when I arrive – St Lucia is a lovely little town, and my guesthouse is friendly and cute (the pool is too cold to go in though).

Esmé, the owner warns me not to walk around the park

behind the house after dark. The railings don't look like they'd provide much protection, but she explains that they're to keep the hippos out. Yes, the most dangerous animal in Africa depending on how you look at it, is the most dangerous animal here because they come out at night and eat. (There are actually "Beware of the Hippo" signs here). (There are also crocodiles, which sometimes come up out of the river at night). There's a lagoon where they live, where there are boat trips in the day, and then the beach where they also play sometimes. I decide to walk up on over to the beach, it's not that far and I figure I have plenty of time.

  It seems a lot further when I'm walking than it did on the map, the sides of the road are lush vegetation which makes it all feel a lot wilder. I finally see the beach car park. People are hanging out, partying, in their cars, BBQs are going. I can't help noting that once again I am the only white person here. It's getting dark faster than I expected, I'm going to have to head back, well now, but I ask a lady in her car where exactly the beach is. "Just over the dunes," she says. I hesitate. "You're basically here," she says, "just go over a bit." She gives me this look and I don't quite get it. In Mexico on the buses I'd get this other look, at first I thought it was 'What's this white girl doing on the bus?' and then I realised it was 'Is this white girl on the right bus?' This look? Feels like pity, like she knows something I don't. What I'd call the poor bastard look. It makes me nervous but maybe I'm misreading her.

I make it to the beach, the waves are insane. Okay, I saw the beach, now I need to dash back to the guesthouse before it gets dark. As I turn there's a white couple walking towards me. They have huge grins on their faces – they've just driven coast to coast from Namibia where they live and work (they're English) to this beach.

I pass back by the lady who directed me to the beach, there's a guy with her now. He smiles and gives me a fist bump, respect for walking around by yourself. Still not sure it's a good idea.

Then I go, looking up at the sun, we're in a race now, and I'm not sure I can make it back in time, I'm also not sure if I'm more scared of the crocodiles, hippos, or strange men in cars. I hear a car pull up behind me, but my instincts don't go off. It's the white couple from the beach, "Do you want a lift?"

"Yes please." Thank God for angels in strange places when I've bitten off more than I can chew.

I am surviving… Esmé recommends going for a later tour – she says the hippos are grumpier early in the morning as they've usually been up all night eating, but I want to get going, I'm in love with South Africa and want to make the most of it, I might even drive up to Jo'burg and do one more safari night at Pilanesberg which, like Ngorongo has volcanic walls. I would like to see a lion.

As I'm leaving she asks how I'm brave enough to go to the beach alone.

"Is it the black and white thing?" I ask, because I still don't think I understand South Africa.

"No," she says, "I don't even think about that. It's being on your own. I'd be embarrassed."

We each have our own fears.

St Lucia

It's a slow riverboat, and we're blessed by "teenage" hippos that don't want to go to sleep and are messing about play fighting and annoying their parents. It's way past their bedtime.

We slide down a smaller part of the river; a croc's favourite spot to sun itself and spot several, and our eagle eyed skipper spots a baby in the reeds. Crocodiles are dedicated mothers he tells us, but if they're getting hungry they'll eat some of their young in order to get by.

The lagoon is home to hippo, crocodiles and the shark responsible for more human deaths than any other - the bull shark (or Zambezi shark as it's known in Africa). The lagoon has been closed off to the sea for 10 years, normally the sharks would get out a bit.

Another inhabitant of this lagoon is the Goliath or Giant

Heron, (the largest heron in the world). One swoops down and lands dangerously close to a crocodile, our skipper can't quite believe it and he's on edge, scared the heron's going to be snapped up.

An African Fish Eagle also shows up. Well, it wouldn't be right if a fish eagle didn't show up for a boat trip.

As I leave the car park I decline to give the guy who's been "watching my car" a tip. The look he gives me makes me think twice. I think I just crossed a cultural line. In England a guy asking for a tip for watching your car is to be ignored, here I think I was supposed to be generous. I am brought back to the Khenpo (senior monk) in Bhutan explaining the difference between charity and generosity, I need to figure out what generosity means here. I'm going to tip the gas station attendants better, they're so nice and helpful and, honestly, I hate pumping my own gas – I'm really grateful for their help.

The only things that call to me here, aside from Pilanesberg right back over the other side of Johannesburg, are the Zulu place (you can stay there too or just watch the show,) which is on the other side of Durban and back up towards Jo'burg, (quite near Pietermaritzburg where Gandhi was famously put off a train because he wasn't allowed in the first class compartment because he was Indian – there's a statue) and something I've discovered in a local St Lucia tourist magazine – the Chief Albert Luthuli Museum. I can't believe

I've never heard of him before, he was the first African to ever receive the Nobel Peace Prize, in 1961. The museum has started with nothing more than his home, all his other work was destroyed or banned in South Africa. It's also the anniversary of his death – 50 years. (Later I discover 2017 was also the 50th anniversary of the first human heart transplant in the world – performed in Cape Town by Dr Christiaan Barnard. The patient survived for 18 days before succumbing to double pneumonia because of the immunosuppressant drugs. And 50 years since the release of The Beatles "Sergeant Pepper's Lonely Hearts Club Band".)

Sometimes I look things up online when I stop for lunch or coffee, sometimes I hear it on the radio, sometimes I drive by a sign that announces an anniversary, a quote.

Chief Luthuli gives me the answer to something that's been bothering me; why am I not at peace? If I can meditate and find joy and feel alive and love all beings, if I have discovered forgiveness, truth, courage, compassion, unconditional love and the ability to take only what I need, then why am I not at peace in myself?

"There can be no peace in any part of the world where there are people oppressed."

And there it is. There's so much more to this man's legacy, so much more that even his own museum, set up in his once home, is struggling to piece together from anecdotes, memories, scraps of work flung out to the world to save it from destruction here, and yet this one phrase lands in my heart, flutters down like a note from the heavens, and I find peace that I cannot be in peace. I can go anywhere I want except home, so am I really free?

It is also 40 years since the murder of Steve Biko. What do I know of Biko other than the song Peter Gabriel sang about him while we danced round our living room in order to free Nelson Mandela? What do I know of him except the title of the film "Cry Freedom"?

I think I knew he was killed by police brutality, but it is also on the radio so maybe I just learn it now (in checking my facts for this book I will discover that he was in fact killed by a brain bleed and subsequent kidney failure which chills me because of my own brother's stroke and kidney failure). On this journey the quote of his that rings around my head as a gong tuning me to my true self, to my soul, is this:

"The most potent weapon in the hands of the oppressor is the mind of the oppressed."

And that is it, even some of the most spiritual teachers of our time are still teaching lies – inferiority to oneself. "You need this coach, this practice, this book, this religion, this meditation practice, you need to do what I say in order to succeed."

In some ways I do it myself; "You will never be free

unless you forgive". I believe this is what Jesus meant when he said "I am the Way", why we call the Camino de Santiago "The Way", it is not the only path, there is not one way to walk it, it has different destinations; Santiago, Finisterre, Muxia, but it is the principles we have to adhere to in order to find healing, freedom and peace. We have to let go, we have to forgive and, as Jesus said in The Sermon on the Mount, we have to let go of judgment of our brother – we have to seek to remove the plank in our own eye before we try to remove the speck of dust in another's.

I have also learned, through Buddhism and all kinds of situations, even this recent debacle with my family, this does not mean to allow someone to walk all over you, to abuse you.

When we abuse ourselves, others, or nature or allow others to abuse us it hurts us all.

I wish I'd run away sooner. It's something I understood after years of wondering why the Dalai Lama fled Tibet when another Buddhist monk or someone like Gandhi might sit down and wait to be arrested (or worse). I found the answer in "The Book of Joy" from the Dalai Lama and Archbishop Desmond Tutu... if he had stayed and been confined or killed, it would have sparked retaliation from the Buddhists and others who supported him. To stay would have led to massacres, so his decision to flee was made in order to avoid conflict. In his book he talks of the Buddhist monk who reached a crisis point in prison, because, while being mistreated he said he was on the verge of losing compassion for his jailors.

Which, of course, brings me to Nelson Mandela.

It was Martin Luther King Jr. who said, *"Hate is too great a burden to bear."* So he set it down and embraced love.

It was Nelson Mandela who saw the man who takes away another's freedom as a prisoner of hatred himself.

It was Nelson Mandela who talked of the bars of prejudice and narrow-mindedness.

It was Nelson Mandela who performed alchemy in those decades in prison, turning hate into compassion, into love for a brother no matter what colour. Who turned a fight for the emancipation of those who had been disempowered into a movement to emancipate all people from a disastrous distribution of power.

"It was during those long and lonely years that my hunger for the freedom of my own people became a hunger for the freedom of all people, white and black. I knew as well as I knew anything that the oppressor must be liberated just as surely as the oppressed".

I miss the turning for the museum, come off, gas up and wait patiently while the attendant decides to wash my windscreen. I tip him well, before I get back on the road and realise I'm just not going to make it there as well as up to see the Zulu dancers. I book it down to PheZulu just in time for the last show of the day. I am the only person in the audience (I think it's lucky when another couple show up, until they start messing with their phones).

The Zulu Dancers - PheZulu

The show is incredible, they dance as if the stands were full. They also teach me about the Zulu way of life, the courting and about the sangoma – the shaman or wise person of the tribe. Before a person becomes a sangoma they are called by the ancestors. They tell me this as I look out over the mountains and soaring birds. Yes, I know I have been called by the ancestors. When they finish I tell them that I too am a dancer, and that I know what it's like when there are not many in the audience and I tell them that they danced for a hundred people and made me feel like a hundred people.

The Gandhi Moment – Near Pietermaritzburg

It's time to hit the road and see how far I can get before it starts to get dark. I almost make it to Pietermaritzburg – the town famous for being the place Gandhi was put off a train, because he wouldn't move to third class. Some say it was the moment his course changed and he became committed to fighting racial oppression, where he developed Satyagraha, his system of peaceful resistance which translates as holding firmly to the truth.

Protea Hotel by Marriott Hilton

I book another Protea hotel, which is completely different to the one in Durban, but nice enough. They're a bit nonplussed when I venture outside onto the road to look at the sunset, and cars slow down to see a white pedestrian, but it's worth it.

I think I can handle the drive to Johannesburg, so I call my car hire company to switch the drop off and they say that's fine, but there'll be a charge at Jo'burg airport when I drop it back. It's about a hundred pounds, which I could easily spend on the flight.

I book the Black Rhino Game Lodge in Pilanesberg – it looks awesome and Pilanesberg has volcanic walls like Ngorongo, so although I haven't made it there yet, I'm hoping this will be as memorable as my trip to Leopard Mountain.

From being underwhelmed a few days into my stay in South Africa, I've fallen passionately in love with it.

\|/

(For the story of the rest of my South Africa trip read my sister Pearl Escapes guide to Johannesburg.)

How I Got There and Getting Around

Crucial Information

Please check the UK government website for safety advice, especially advice on where it is safe to pick up hire cars, and whether it is safe to use Uber or other non-hotel/official taxis and cars, as unfortunately, shortly after I travelled Uber drivers were being targeted and their cars burnt out by competitors in Johannesburg.

I flew from London Heathrow to Johannesburg OR Tambo with British Airways for £367.

I took an official taxi from the airport to Pretoria.

I took a hotel car to visit the Mandela Statue.

I took an Uber to Maropeng.

I took a hotel car and driver to Soweto and on to the airport.

I flew to Durban (again via BA, booked at their desk in Johannesburg airport), where I used various taxis and hotel taxis and then hired a car from Hertz. I have since had to request a refund for monies charged over a year later (it might be useful to cancel your credit card on your return and get a new one to avoid any credit card shenanigans).

I drove back to Johannesburg (during the day).

\|/

Nowadays I use the following resources to get from A to B – each of these may be 100% accurate at times, but don't count on it:-

www.rome2rio.com – how to get anywhere – extremely useful.

Google Maps – if you use the walk or public transport function to look at your distance to destination you will often get some unusual and useful suggestions, but do not trust this one blindly – always verify with another source.

Trainline – excellent for trains in the UK, also gives coach options, however UK coaches are a law unto themselves with bus drivers often giving differing advice depending on their mood.

Local advice – this can include tourist information, hotel and guesthouse hosts, as well as any local person. Remember that in many parts of the world the locals do not use public transport, but rely instead on cars, so may not be aware that certain services exist or have changed.

Bus timetables – sometimes these are really out of date – don't make assumptions – and always double check that there is a bus or train back before you go too far!

Kayak – if you use the nearby airport option you may be surprised by what turns up!

Expedia also often has flights that don't show up on

Kayak.

For South East Asia check the airline website directly to see all available flights (likewise Virgin flights are often hidden on third party booking websites.)

If you like to speak to someone, calling Virgin to book is an extremely pleasant experience.

The Google flight tool is also excellent and the map makes nearby options easier to spot.

Sadly booking flights and trains seems to be getting more complicated and so splitting your ticket (or jumping off halfway through – not in the middle of the ocean but at a connecting airport) is an option if you have hand luggage only.

The Details and the Rest

Safety

If you have a driver at any point get their advice on local and national customs and safety advice. I was advised:

- do not drive at night and be careful of service stations around Johannesburg

- if you are going to hire a car don't do it in Johannesburg as tourists are targeted for car jacking

- do not walk around unless you know it is safe to do so, be more wary at night, especially in areas with the hippo signs (there may also be crocodiles hunting at night)

- do not swim unless you know it is safe to do so

- do not sleep on your terrace in a game park as leopards eat people

- do not trust your satnav, GPS or Google maps – get directions and maps

- there is a level of credit card fraud so be careful of where you use your card and check bank statements

Places to Stay (Durban and Surrounding Area)

The Best – Food, Massage, Service, Room and Tour – just out of this world:

Leopard Mountain Safari Lodge, D464 District Road, 3960 Mkuze, South Africa £226 including afternoon tea, dinner, breakfast, evening game drive, morning game drive, complimentary booze in the hotel room, cocktails on the evening game drive, hot chocolate on the morning game drive and, if memory serves, tea, coffee and goodies throughout, did not include massage, via Booking.com

Also, places en route and for other tours:

Coastlands Musgrave Hotel, 315 - 319 Peter Mokaba Ridge , Musgrave, 4001 Durban £63 not including breakfast via Booking.com

Protea Hotel by Marriott Durban Umhlanga, Corner Lighthouse Road & Chartwell Road, Umhlanga Rocks, Umhlanga, 4001 Durban, South Africa £63 not including breakfast via Booking.com

The Sandpiper Guesthouse, 17 Sandpiper Street, St Lucia, 3936 South Africa

Protea Hotel by Marriott Hilton near Pietermaritzburg

Places to Stay (Johannesburg and Surrounding Area)

Coral Tree Inn, 69 Korannaberg Road, Waterkloof Heights, 0181 Pretoria £55 including breakfast via Booking.com

Maropeng Boutique Hotel, Maropeng R400, just off R563 to Hekpoort, Cradle of Humankind, 1751 Magaliesburg £59 including breakfast via Booking.com

Black Rhino Game Lodge, s/n Pilanesberg National Park, North West Province, 0001 Pilanesberg, South Africa £189 including lunch, dinner, breakfast, evening game drive and morning game drive via Booking.com

Language

Eleven official languages, English is one of them, thank goodness. There are said to be 35 languages spoken in the country.

Visa

Those with a UK passport do not need a visa. Check the UK government website for passport validity and lengths of stay (90 days without a visa is the general length of time allowed).

Currency

South African rand (ZAR) - exchange rate, around 20 to a UK pound.

Time Difference

1 hour ahead of London time.

Tipping

Similar to the US; US$1 or 10-15 ZAR per day for hotel staff, porters, 10-15% in restaurants. It's also common to tip service station assistants who wash your windscreen etc. when filling up your tank (whether you want them to or not). Some locals will also ask for a tip when you return to the car park as they have "watched" your car for you – best to ask local advice as to whether this is appropriate and/or to be encouraged.

Safari lodges will often provide envelopes for tips, which can be for your overall stay or for individuals who have made your stay special (usually the guides!) Don't be afraid to ask at reception what is customary and tip according to the experience you've had.

Some tour companies will have a small notice either saying that tips are included or are appreciated, (if not included 10% of the total charge would be a good tip). Most of the tours

I took were by official park guides so they did not accept tips.

Toilets

Most restaurants, service stations and large monuments/sites have decent loos.

Further Reading

"The Long Walk To Freedom" – Nelson Mandela audio book narrated by Danny Glover

"The Book of Joy" – His Holiness the Dalai Lama and Archbishop Desmond Tutu with Douglas Abrams

"Born A Crime" – Trevor Noah audio book (essential listening)

"Man's Search For Meaning" – Viktor E. Frankl

"Cry Freedom" – film (not seen)

Playlist

"You're The Voice" – John Farnham

"Something Inside So Strong" – Labi Siffre

"Biko" – Peter Gabriel

"La Fantastica" – Zumba Fitness, ZIN 51

"Boujé" – J Perry, ZIN 47

"Zoomer" – Les Jumo, ZIN Mega Mix 25

"Got 2 Luv U" – Sean Paul (feat. Alexis Jordan)

"Mamafrikalo" – ZIN Mega Mix 38

"Maputo Song" – Maputo Drummers

"Wololo" – Rose Muhando

About the Author

I'm Pearl. When I came up with the concept of Pearl Escapes, as well as the escape in a box, my goal was to share all of the wonderful things I was discovering, especially spas, with everyone around the world. At the time I gave myself the tongue in cheek title of Explorer-in-Chief, and it stuck.

Over the nine years since then, I realised that I was really sharing healing, I've tried over 500 types, and my 2019 book is, I believe, the most complete guide to forms of healing in the world. Ultimately what I do is simply to help people feel alive and, although this path challenges me at times, I have the greatest reward for doing this; whenever I get lost and stop following the beat of my own drum – whenever I start trying to be someone that I'm not, the universe puts me, one way or another, back on my path and makes me feel alive again.

Please do check out all the books I've written as I really hope, especially in the healing guide, that there is something there for every single person around the world who is hurting, healing or just comfortably numb. I have learned, over the last nine years, that whether we walk alone or dance at a convention, we heal together, because as any spiritual guru worth their salt will tell you – we are all connected.

Buen camino!

\|/

For more check out www.pearlescapes.co.uk or follow me on Instagram @pearlescapes (I am on Facebook, Twitter and LinkedIn but Instagram is home).

Oh and don't forget I'm a real person and you can email me, pearl@pearlescapes.co.uk - I love hearing your stories too.

Thank You

Thank you for buying and reading this book, I made it just for you.

And thank you to all the many people, places and animals who have helped me on my journey – thank you for taking care of me, thank you for loving me.

Ingram Content Group UK Ltd.
Milton Keynes UK
UKHW011814280623
424207UK00001B/152